Make Sh** Happen

Delegate like a Boss

Deborah LeBlanc, CCHt, CAHA

Table of Contents

Introduction

Delegation, the art of entrusting tasks and initiatives to other capable hands within your team, is akin to orchestrating a symphony where each member plays a vital part. It's not only about offloading work; rather, it's a strategic maneuver aimed at optimizing resources and fostering collective success.

A leader, burdened with way too many responsibilities, can realize the necessity of redistributing tasks. It's not a sign of weakness but rather a testament to astute leadership. Delegation is the cornerstone of effective management, a skill that separates great leaders from merely good ones.

Picture yourself at the helm of a team, each member possessing unique talents and strengths. You, as the leader, hold the blueprint of the collective vision. However, realizing this vision requires more than just your individual efforts. It demands capitalizing on the collective potential of your team through effective delegation.

At its core, delegation is about empowerment. It's about recognizing the capabilities of your team members and entrusting them with responsibilities that align with their skills, interests, and aspirations. By doing so, you not only lighten your own load but also nurture a culture of trust and collaboration within your team.

Consider the impact of effective delegation on both personal and team productivity. When you strategically assign tasks, you free up valuable time to focus on high-impact work that moves the needle forward. Meanwhile, your team members are given the opportunity to delve into projects that pique their curiosity and challenge their abilities, leading to enhanced engagement and job satisfaction.

Furthermore, delegation serves as a powerful tool for skill development and professional growth. When you delegate tasks, you're not just handing off work; you're providing learning opportunities for your team members to expand their capabilities and broaden their horizons. It's a win-win situation where both the individual and the team stand to benefit from the exchange.

But effective delegation is also about promoting a culture of accountability and ownership. When team members are entrusted with responsibilities, they feel a sense of pride and ownership in their work, driving them to deliver results with excellence and diligence.

So how will we proceed in this book? First and foremost, we'll lay the foundation by exploring the essence of delegation and its pivotal role in effective leadership. From dispelling common misconceptions to understanding the profound impact of delegation on personal and team productivity, you'll gain a comprehensive understanding of this essential skill.

But this isn't just about passive learning. Throughout the book, you'll be challenged to put theory into practice. We'll introduce various exercises and techniques to help you assess your delegation strengths and weaknesses, encouraging you to reflect on past experiences where delegation proved instrumental in achieving success.

Next, we'll dive into the nitty-gritty of delegation and explore practical strategies for building trust, fostering autonomy, and setting clear expectations. You'll learn how to harness the diverse talents within your team and allocate tasks effectively, paving the way for seamless collaboration and maximum productivity.

But theory alone won't suffice. It's time to roll up your sleeves and get your hands dirty. We'll provide actionable tips on how to delegate with purpose, avoiding common pitfalls such as micromanagement and over-delegation. Through practice and refinement, you'll hone your delegation skills like a seasoned leader.

Of course, no journey is without its challenges. We'll address the roadblocks and obstacles that may hinder your delegation progress, from overcoming the fear of losing control to managing conflicts within your team. By creating a supportive environment and prioritizing open communication, you'll navigate these hurdles with confidence and grace.

As we conclude our journey, we leave you with a powerful message: delegation isn't just about distributing tasks—it's about empowering your team to achieve their full potential.

Are you ready to unlock the transformative power of delegation and propel your team to new heights of success? Then dive in, and let's master the art of delegation together.

Chapter One

Put Together a Powerhouse Team

Welcome to the first chapter of *Delegate like a Boss*—your guide to mastering the art of delegation and cultivating a powerhouse team. In this journey toward effective leadership, we'll explore how to assemble a team that not only supports your vision but propels it to new heights.

Picture this: you're at the helm of your organization, facing a variety of tasks and responsibilities. While it may be tempting to shoulder the burden alone, true leadership lies in empowering others. That's where delegation comes in—it's not just about assigning tasks but about building a team that thrives on collaboration and innovation.

Throughout this chapter, we'll delve into the heart of delegation, uncovering its essence and unraveling its potential to transform your leadership journey. Together, we'll learn how to navigate the challenges of delegation, overcome common misconceptions, and unlock the full potential of your team.

Understand Delegation

What Is Delegation?

Delegation is the strategic process through which leaders entrust tasks and responsibilities to others within their team or organization. It goes beyond simply assigning tasks; it involves empowering individuals to take ownership and contribute to the achievement of collective goals. Delegation is about leveraging the diverse skills and talents of team members, allowing leaders to focus on high-priority activities that align with organizational objectives. It fosters a culture of collaboration, innovation, and accountability by distributing tasks effectively and providing opportunities for growth and development.

Effective delegation requires clear communication, understanding of team members' strengths, and establishing mechanisms for accountability and support. As a result, delegation enables leaders to optimize their time and resources, driving productivity and efficiency while nurturing a dynamic and empowered team.

Why Delegation Matters

Delegation is not merely a convenience for leaders; it is an essential ingredient for organizational success. Its significance lies in its ability to unlock the full potential of both leaders and team members. Delegation allows leaders to leverage the diverse skills, talents, and perspectives of their team, leading to more innovative solutions and better outcomes. By distributing tasks effectively, leaders can focus their time and energy on strategic initiatives that drive the organization forward, rather than getting bogged down in day-to-day operational tasks.

When team members are entrusted with responsibilities, they feel valued and motivated to perform at their best. This sense of ownership not only increases job satisfaction but also encourages individuals to take the initiative and contribute their ideas and expertise to the organization's success.

Furthermore, delegation is crucial for leadership development. By delegating tasks, leaders provide opportunities for their team members to learn new skills, take on greater responsibilities, and grow professionally. This not only benefits the individual but also strengthens the overall capabilities of the team.

Delegation also enhances organizational agility and resilience. In today's fast-paced and dynamic business environment, organizations need to be adaptable and responsive to change. Delegation allows for better resource allocation and decision-making, enabling organizations to navigate challenges more effectively and seize opportunities more quickly.

Key Elements of Delegation

Effective delegation relies on several foundational elements that ensure tasks are assigned and executed successfully. These elements serve as the building blocks for a structured and efficient delegation process:

- **Clear Communication**: Communication lies at the heart of delegation. Leaders must clearly articulate the tasks, responsibilities, expectations, and desired outcomes to the individuals to whom they are delegating. Clarity in communication minimizes misunderstandings and ensures that everyone is on the same page regarding what needs to be accomplished.

- **Proper Task Allocation**: Properly assigning tasks involves matching the right tasks with the right individuals based on their skills, expertise, and capacity. Leaders should consider the strengths and capabilities of each team member when delegating tasks to ensure that they are positioned for success.

- **Setting Clear Expectations**: Setting clear expectations is essential for successful delegation. Leaders must outline the specific goals, deadlines, and performance standards associated with each delegated task. In turn, clear expectations provide clarity and guidance to the individuals responsible for completing the tasks, helping them understand what is expected of them and what success looks like.

- **Providing Necessary Resources and Support**: Leaders must ensure that team members have access to the resources, tools, information, and support they need to complete their delegated tasks effectively. This may include providing training, guidance, access to technology or equipment, or additional support from other team members or departments.

- **Establishing Mechanisms for Accountability and Feedback**: Accountability is crucial for ensuring that delegated tasks are completed on time and to the desired standard. Leaders should establish clear mechanisms for tracking progress, monitoring performance, and providing feedback on delegated tasks. Regular check-ins, progress reports, and performance reviews help keep everyone accountable and ensure that delegated tasks stay on track.

By adhering to these key elements of delegation, leaders can empower their team members to take ownership of tasks, contribute meaningfully to the organization's goals, and ultimately drive success.

Benefits of Effective Delegation

Effective delegation offers a multitude of benefits for both leaders and team members, contributing to enhanced productivity, job satisfaction, and overall organizational success. Here are some key benefits:

- **Increased Productivity**: Delegation allows leaders to focus their time and energy on strategic tasks and high-priority initiatives, leading to increased productivity and efficiency. By entrusting routine tasks to capable team members, leaders can accomplish more in less time, driving progress and achieving organizational goals more effectively.

- **Empowerment and Development**: Delegation empowers team members by providing them with opportunities to take on new responsibilities, develop new skills, and grow professionally. When individuals are entrusted with tasks and given the autonomy to make decisions, they feel valued and motivated to perform at their best. This sense of empowerment fosters a culture of continuous learning and development within the organization, leading to increased engagement and job satisfaction.

- **Improved Time Management**: Delegation enables leaders to better manage their time and prioritize their workload. By delegating tasks that do not require their specific expertise or attention, leaders can free up valuable time to focus on strategic planning, decision-making, and relationship-building activities that drive long-term success.

- **Enhanced Team Collaboration**: Delegation promotes collaboration and teamwork within the organization. When tasks are distributed among team members based on their skills and expertise, it encourages them to work together, share knowledge, and support each other in achieving common goals. This collaborative approach encourages a sense of camaraderie and unity among team members, leading to improved communication, creativity, and problem-solving abilities.

- **Leadership Development Opportunities**: Effective delegation is a key component of leadership development. By delegating tasks and responsibilities, leaders provide opportunities for their team members to develop their leadership skills, decision-making abilities, and problem-solving capabilities. This not only benefits the individual team members but also strengthens the overall leadership capacity of the organization, ensuring its long-term success and sustainability.

- **Improved Work-Life Balance**: Delegation can help alleviate workload pressures and prevent burnout among team members. By redistributing tasks evenly and empowering team members to take ownership of their work, leaders can promote a healthier work-life balance and reduce stress levels within the organization. This leads to higher job satisfaction, increased morale, and lower turnover rates, contributing to a positive and supportive work environment.

Misconceptions About Delegation

Fear of Losing Control

The fear of losing control often inhibits effective delegation. Leaders may worry that relinquishing tasks will result in a loss of authority or quality control. However, by establishing clear expectations, providing adequate support, and fostering open communication, leaders can delegate confidently while maintaining oversight. Trusting in the capabilities of team members and understanding that delegation is a collaborative process can help alleviate this fear. Embracing delegation as a means to empower others and enhance efficiency allows leaders to focus on higher-level responsibilities without micromanaging. Overcoming the fear of losing control requires a shift in mindset toward viewing delegation as a tool for shared success rather than a loss of power.

Doubt in Others' Abilities

Doubt in others' abilities arises when leaders question whether team members possess the necessary skills or expertise to successfully complete delegated tasks. This doubt can stem from a lack of trust or familiarity with team members' capabilities. However, leaders must recognize that effective delegation involves assessing and leveraging the strengths of each team member. Overcoming doubt in others' abilities requires proactive steps such as providing training, resources, and guidance to support team members in their assigned tasks. Additionally, leaders can delegate tasks gradually, starting with smaller responsibilities and gradually increasing the complexity as trust and confidence in the team members grow. By offering constructive feedback and recognizing achievements along the way, leaders can instill confidence in their team members and empower them to succeed. Thus, embracing a mindset of trust and collaboration is essential for overcoming doubt in others' abilities and fostering a culture of empowerment within the team.

Concerns about Perception

Concerns about perception usually hinder effective delegation as leaders worry about how they will be perceived by their team, peers, or superiors. They may fear being seen as lazy, incompetent, or lacking leadership skills if they delegate too much or too often. However, it's crucial for leaders to understand that delegation is a strategic decision aimed at optimizing productivity and leveraging the collective talents of the team. Overcoming concerns about perception involves reframing delegation as a sign of strength rather than weakness. Leaders should communicate openly about the reasons for delegation, emphasizing its benefits for both themselves and the team. Additionally, demonstrating trust in team members' abilities and acknowledging their contributions publicly can help dispel any negative perceptions. Therefore, by focusing on results and the overall success of the team, leaders can overcome concerns about perception and create a culture that values delegation as a key aspect of effective leadership.

Debunking Common Myths

Debunking common myths surrounding delegation is essential for leaders to embrace their full potential without unnecessary hesitations. One prevalent myth is that delegation equates to passing off work to others without taking responsibility. In reality, effective delegation involves careful planning, clear communication, and accountability. Another myth is that delegation is only suitable for menial tasks, while in truth, it can encompass a wide range of responsibilities, including strategic decision-making. Moreover, some believe that delegation is a sign of weakness or incompetence, but in reality, it is a hallmark of effective leadership, enabling leaders to focus on high-impact tasks and develop their team members. So debunking these myths and understanding the true nature and benefits of delegation, leaders can unlock its transformative power and drive organizational success.

Unlocking the Hidden Potential

Leverage Skills and Talents

At the heart of effective delegation lies the art of recognizing and harnessing the unique skills and talents within a team. Each member possesses a distinct set of strengths waiting to be utilized. Effective leaders understand that tapping into these abilities isn't just about task assignment; it's about strategic alignment. By keenly observing team dynamics and individual capabilities, leaders can match tasks with the right individuals, fostering an environment where everyone excels. This approach optimizes productivity and nurtures a culture of empowerment and growth. When individuals are entrusted with tasks that resonate with their skills and passions, they feel valued and motivated to deliver their best. In turn, when you, as the leader, leverage the diverse talents of your team, you can unlock unprecedented levels of creativity, innovation, and success.

Prioritize Tasks

Effective delegation hinges on the strategic prioritization of tasks. Not all tasks are equally suited for delegation; some require specialized skills or expertise, while others are routine or administrative in nature. Leaders must assess the importance, complexity, and urgency of each task to determine which ones can be delegated without compromising quality or outcomes. Prioritizing tasks for delegation involves identifying those that align with the strengths and capabilities of team members while freeing up valuable time for leaders to focus on strategic initiatives. By delegating tasks strategically, leaders can ensure that resources are allocated efficiently and that the most critical objectives receive the attention they deserve. This approach not only enhances productivity and efficiency but also empowers team members to take on greater responsibilities and contribute meaningfully to the organization's success.

Spot Opportunities

Spotting opportunities for delegation requires a nuanced approach. It involves a strategic assessment of tasks and projects, aiming to identify areas where team members can excel and contribute meaningfully. Rather than viewing delegation as a reactive measure, leaders should proactively seek out opportunities to distribute responsibilities. This involves considering the complexity, time sensitivity, and skill requirements of each task. By understanding the strengths and capabilities of their team members, leaders can match tasks with individuals who are best suited to handle them. Moreover, spotting opportunities for delegation also entails recognizing tasks that provide valuable growth opportunities for team members, allowing them to develop new skills and expand their expertise. Therefore, embracing a proactive mindset toward delegation enables leaders to optimize resource allocation, foster skill development, and drive overall team effectiveness and success.

Boost Efficiency

Delegation serves as a powerful tool for enhancing efficiency within teams and organizations. By entrusting tasks to individuals with the appropriate skills and capabilities, leaders can streamline processes, accelerate decision-making, and maximize productivity. Boosting efficiency through delegation involves a systematic approach to task allocation, ensuring that each team member is assigned tasks aligned with their strengths and expertise. This not only optimizes workflow but also reduces the burden on leaders, freeing up time for strategic planning and high-impact initiatives. Delegation also fosters a culture of empowerment and accountability, as team members take ownership of their assigned tasks and strive for excellence. Leaders should provide clear guidance, support, and feedback throughout the delegation process to ensure smooth execution and desired outcomes. So by leveraging delegation as a means to enhance efficiency, organizations can achieve their goals more effectively and adapt to changing demands in today's dynamic business environment.

Ways of Enhancing Leadership

Build Trust in Your Team

Building trust in your team is the cornerstone of effective leadership. Trust is the currency of successful delegation, as it lays the foundation for open communication, collaboration, and mutual respect. Leaders cultivate trust by demonstrating transparency, integrity, and consistency in their actions. They empower team members by delegating tasks that align with their strengths and providing opportunities for growth and development. By entrusting individuals with responsibilities and showing confidence in their abilities, leaders foster a sense of ownership and accountability within the team. Moreover, building trust involves actively listening to team members, valuing their input, and addressing their concerns. When trust is established, team members feel empowered to take the initiative, make decisions, and contribute their best work, ultimately driving success for the entire organization.

Set Clear Expectations

Setting clear expectations is essential for effective delegation and team performance. Leaders must articulate the desired outcomes, timelines, and quality standards for delegated tasks. Clear expectations provide clarity and direction, ensuring that team members understand what is expected of them and how their contributions align with organizational goals. Additionally, setting clear expectations helps prevent misunderstandings and reduces the likelihood of errors or delays in task completion. Leaders should communicate expectations openly and proactively, allowing team members to ask questions and seek clarification as needed. Also, leaders should be specific in their instructions and provide relevant context to help team members understand the importance and impact of their assigned tasks. By setting clear expectations, leaders empower their team members to work autonomously, make informed decisions, and deliver results that exceed expectations.

Provide Support and Resources

Effective delegation goes hand in hand with providing adequate support and resources to ensure the success of delegated tasks. Leaders should equip their team members with the tools, information, and assistance needed to fulfill their responsibilities effectively. This may include providing access to training programs, relevant documentation, or technical support. Additionally, leaders should offer guidance and mentorship to help team members navigate challenges and overcome obstacles that may arise during task execution. By offering continuous support, leaders demonstrate their commitment to the success and development of their team members, fostering a culture of trust and collaboration. Moreover, providing resources such as time, budget, and manpower demonstrates organizational investment in the delegated tasks, further motivating team members to perform at their best.

Changing Mindsets

Shift Perspectives on Delegation

Delegation is often misunderstood as a means of offloading tasks or relinquishing control. However, its true essence lies in its potential to transform the dynamics of leadership and team collaboration. Shifting perspectives on delegation requires a fundamental reevaluation of its purpose and benefits. Instead of viewing delegation as a sign of weakness or incompetence, recognize it as a strategic tool for maximizing efficiency and unleashing the full potential of your team.

Adopt the idea that effective delegation is not about relinquishing control but about empowering others to take ownership and excel in their roles. By distributing tasks based on individual strengths and expertise, leaders can foster a culture of trust, accountability, and innovation within their teams.

Furthermore, shifting perspectives on delegation involves reframing it as a means of personal and professional growth. Rather than seeing it as a burden, view delegation as an opportunity to develop leadership skills, build stronger relationships with team members, and focus on high-impact initiatives that drive organizational success.

Embrace a Growth Mindset

Embracing a growth mindset is essential for effective delegation and personal development. A growth mindset is characterized by the belief that abilities and intelligence can be developed through dedication and effort. When it comes to delegation, a growth mindset enables leaders to see challenges as opportunities for learning and growth, rather than obstacles to be avoided. Leaders with a growth mindset are open to feedback, willing to take risks, and resilient in the face of setbacks.

To embrace a growth mindset, leaders should cultivate a mindset of continuous improvement and adaptability. They should encourage experimentation and innovation within their teams, recognizing that failure is not a sign of incompetence but an essential part of the learning process. By fostering a culture of learning and growth, leaders empower their team members to stretch beyond their comfort zones, take on new challenges, and reach their full potential.

Adopting a growth mindset also involves reframing setbacks and failures as opportunities for growth and development. Instead of viewing them as evidence of inadequacy, leaders should see them as valuable learning experiences that provide insights and lessons for future success.

Overcome Resistance to Delegation

Resistance to delegation is a common barrier that leaders must address to foster effective teamwork and productivity. This resistance can stem from various sources, including fear of losing control, lack of trust in team members' abilities, or reluctance to relinquish tasks. To overcome resistance to delegation, leaders must first understand the root causes and address them proactively.

One approach is to communicate openly with team members about the benefits of delegation, such as increased autonomy, skill development, and opportunities for growth. Leaders should emphasize that delegation is not about micromanagement or relinquishing control but about empowering team members to take ownership and contribute meaningfully to the organization's success.

Additionally, leaders can build trust and confidence in their team members by providing training, support, and recognition for their efforts. By demonstrating faith in their capabilities and offering guidance when needed, leaders can help alleviate concerns and build a culture of trust and collaboration.

Moreover, leaders should be mindful of their own mindset and behaviors toward delegation. They should lead by example, delegating tasks effectively and communicating openly about expectations and responsibilities.

Develop a Delegation Strategy

Crafting a delegation strategy is essential for leaders to effectively distribute tasks and empower their team members. A delegation strategy involves identifying tasks that can be delegated, assessing team members' strengths and capabilities, and establishing clear guidelines and expectations for task execution.

To develop a delegation strategy, leaders should start by conducting a comprehensive assessment of their workload and identifying tasks that can be delegated without compromising quality or outcomes. They should consider factors such as complexity, time sensitivity, and skill requirements when determining which tasks to delegate.

Next, leaders should assess the strengths and capabilities of their team members to ensure that tasks are assigned to individuals who are best suited to handle them. They should consider factors such as expertise, experience, and workload when matching tasks with team members.

Once tasks have been assigned, leaders should establish clear guidelines and expectations for task execution. This includes defining the desired outcomes, timelines, and quality standards for each task, as well as providing necessary resources and support to ensure success.

Leaders should maintain open communication channels with team members throughout the delegation process, providing feedback, guidance, and encouragement as needed. By developing a delegation strategy that is tailored to the needs of their team and organization, leaders can optimize productivity, and drive overall success.

The Ripple Effect

Impact on Team Morale

Effective delegation has a profound impact on team morale, shaping the overall atmosphere and productivity within an organization. When leaders delegate tasks thoughtfully and empower team members to take on responsibilities, it fosters a sense of trust, autonomy, and ownership among the team.

One of the key ways delegation impacts team morale is by boosting confidence and motivation. When individuals are entrusted with tasks and given the opportunity to showcase their abilities, it validates their skills and capabilities, leading to increased self-esteem and confidence. This sense of accomplishment and recognition fuels motivation and encourages team members to go above and beyond in their roles.

Delegation also promotes a sense of belonging and collaboration within the team. When individuals are actively involved in decision-making and task execution, it fosters a collective sense of ownership and accountability for the team's success. This creates a supportive environment where team members feel valued, respected, and appreciated for their contributions.

Furthermore, effective delegation can help alleviate feelings of overwhelm and burnout among team members. By distributing tasks evenly and leveraging the diverse skills and talents of the team, leaders prevent individuals from feeling overburdened or stretched thin. This promotes a healthier work-life balance and reduces stress levels, leading to higher morale and job satisfaction.

On the other hand, poor delegation practices, such as micromanagement or overloading individuals with tasks beyond their capacity, can have a detrimental impact on team morale. It can lead to feelings of frustration, demotivation, and disengagement among team members, ultimately hindering productivity and collaboration.

Organizational Benefits of Delegation

Delegation isn't just beneficial for individual leaders and team members; it also offers significant advantages for the organization as a whole. By effectively delegating tasks and responsibilities, organizations can unlock a host of benefits that contribute to their overall success and sustainability.

First and foremost, delegation enhances organizational efficiency and productivity. When leaders distribute tasks among team members based on their skills and expertise, it optimizes resource allocation and enables tasks to be completed more efficiently. This allows the organization to accomplish more in less time, leading to increased productivity and better outcomes.

Second, delegation fosters a culture of empowerment and employee engagement within the organization. When individuals are entrusted with responsibilities and given the autonomy to make decisions, they feel valued and motivated to perform at their best. This leads to higher levels of job satisfaction, morale, and retention, ultimately contributing to a positive work environment and a more engaged workforce.

Delegation also promotes leadership development and succession planning within the organization. By providing opportunities for team members to take on new responsibilities and grow their skills and expertise, delegation helps cultivate a pipeline of future leaders. This ensures that the organization has the talent and capabilities needed to thrive in the long term.

Moreover, delegation encourages innovation and creativity within the organization. When individuals are empowered to take ownership of tasks and make decisions, it fosters a culture of experimentation and risk-taking. This leads to new ideas, approaches, and solutions that drive innovation and keep the organization competitive in today's fast-paced business environment.

Empower Others through Delegation

Delegation isn't just about assigning tasks; it's about empowering others to realize their full potential and contribute meaningfully to the organization's success. When leaders delegate effectively, they give their team members the opportunity to take ownership of tasks, make decisions, and develop new skills. This empowerment fosters a sense of ownership and accountability among team members, motivating them to perform at their best.

Delegation builds trust and confidence within the team. When leaders trust their team members to handle delegated tasks, it sends a powerful message that their contributions are valued and respected. This trust strengthens the bond between leaders and team members, creating a supportive environment where everyone feels empowered to take initiative and share their ideas.

Furthermore, empowerment through delegation leads to increased engagement and job satisfaction. When individuals are given the autonomy to make decisions and contribute to the organization's goals, they feel a sense of pride and fulfillment in their work. This leads to higher levels of motivation, morale, and retention, ultimately benefiting the organization as a whole.

So by empowering others through delegation, leaders not only lighten their own workload but also foster a culture of trust, accountability, and growth within the team. This empowers individuals to reach their full potential and drive the organization forward toward success.

Conclusion

In conclusion, delegation emerges as a pivotal aspect of effective leadership and offers a pathway to unlock the full potential of both leaders and team members. Through our exploration of delegation, we've unearthed its transformative power in fostering collaboration, innovation, and accountability within teams.

We've highlighted its role in driving organizational success and enhancing productivity. By embracing key elements such as clear communication, setting expectations, and providing necessary support, leaders lay the foundation for effective delegation and empower their teams to excel.

Moreover, we've addressed common misconceptions surrounding delegation, dispelling fears and doubts that may inhibit its adoption. By debunking these myths and shifting perspectives, leaders can embrace delegation as a strategic tool for growth and development.

Moving forward, it's crucial to leverage the skills and talents within your team, prioritizing tasks for delegation and spotting opportunities for growth. By boosting efficiency through delegation and fostering a culture of collaboration and accountability, leaders enhance their own leadership capabilities while empowering their teams to achieve greatness.

As we conclude this chapter, remember that delegation isn't just about assigning tasks; it's about empowering others to realize their full potential. By encouraging a culture of delegation and accountability, leaders create ripple effects that extend far beyond individual tasks, driving organizational success and fostering a supportive and thriving work environment.

Chapter Two

Celebrate (and Leverage) Differences

In this chapter, we delve into the transformative power of celebrating and leveraging differences within your team. Assembling a team that mirrors the kaleidoscope of the world around us isn't merely a matter of meeting quotas—it's a strategic imperative. It's about recognizing that each individual brings a unique set of skills, insights, and cultural backgrounds to the table, enriching the collective dynamic in ways that transcend traditional boundaries.

We'll explore the profound benefits of recruiting a diverse team, understanding the strengths and experiences of each team member, and fostering a culture of inclusivity where every voice is not only heard but celebrated. We'll also delve into the critical role that trust plays in effective delegation, and how tailoring communication and delegation styles can unlock the full potential of your team.

The Importance of Recruiting Your Team

Assemble a Diverse Team

Imagine a team as diverse as a vibrant mosaic, where each piece contributes a unique hue, texture, and pattern to the overall picture. This is the essence of assembling a diverse team—a dynamic blend of backgrounds, skills, and perspectives that enriches the collective experience and propels the team toward greater heights of success.

Diversity in team composition goes far beyond meeting quotas or ticking boxes—it's about harnessing the power of difference to drive innovation, creativity, and resilience. When individuals from various walks of life come together, they bring with them a wealth of knowledge, insights, and approaches to problem-solving that can't be replicated in homogeneous groups.

Consider the benefits of having a team with members from different cultural backgrounds. Each individual brings a unique worldview shaped by their heritage, traditions, and experiences, offering fresh perspectives and alternative ways of thinking. This diversity of thought sparks creativity and fosters a culture of open-mindedness, where innovative ideas flourish and breakthroughs abound.

Moreover, assembling a diverse team is not just about the skills and experiences that each member brings to the table—it's also about fostering a culture of inclusion and belonging. When team members see themselves reflected in their colleagues and feel valued for their unique contributions, they are more motivated to fully engage with their work and collaborate with their peers.

In today's rapidly evolving world, where complexity is the norm and uncertainty is a constant companion, diversity isn't just a nice-to-have—it's a crucial factor to success. It equips teams with the adaptability, resilience, and creativity needed to navigate challenges and seize opportunities in an ever-changing landscape.

Understand Individual Strengths, Experiences, and Perspectives

In the landscape of modern workplaces, understanding the individual strengths, experiences, and perspectives within your team is akin to unlocking a treasure trove of untapped potential. Each team member brings to the table a unique set of skills, honed through diverse experiences and shaped by personal perspectives.

Imagine a team where one member, with a background in finance, brings a keen eye for detail and analytical prowess to the table, while another, hailing from a creative arts background, infuses the team with innovative thinking and outside-the-box solutions. Yet another team member with a history of customer service brings empathy and interpersonal skills that deepen client relationships and foster trust. These varied backgrounds and perspectives, far from being mere differences, are the building blocks of a cohesive and high-performing team.

By taking the time to truly understand each team member on a personal level, leaders unlock a wealth of potential for effective task assignment and collaboration. They recognize that Sally's penchant for detail makes her the perfect candidate for meticulous data analysis tasks, while John's creative flair lends itself beautifully to brainstorming sessions and problem-solving exercises. Moreover, by embracing diverse perspectives, teams are better equipped to tackle complex challenges from multiple angles, leading to more robust solutions and innovative breakthroughs.

Beyond the immediate benefits to task delegation and problem-solving, promoting an environment where individual strengths and perspectives are valued creates a sense of belonging and empowerment among team members. When individuals feel seen and appreciated for their unique contributions, they are more motivated to actively engage with their work and collaborate with their colleagues. This sense of inclusivity not only enhances team morale but also cultivates a culture of creativity and innovation that propels the team toward greater success.

Create a Culture of Inclusivity

Now, picture a workplace where every voice is not only heard but actively sought after—a place where differences aren't just tolerated but celebrated. In this vibrant ecosystem of inclusivity, every team member feels valued, respected, and empowered to bring their authentic selves to the table. This is the essence of fostering a culture of inclusivity within your team—a culture that transcends superficial differences and embraces the rich tapestry of human experience.

In an inclusive work environment, open lines of communication flow freely, creating a space where ideas are welcomed from all corners. Team members feel comfortable expressing their thoughts and opinions, knowing that they will be met with genuine interest and respect. This fosters a culture of collaboration and innovation, where diverse perspectives converge to generate creative solutions to even the most complex challenges.

Moreover, an inclusive culture extends beyond the confines of the workplace, enriching interactions with clients, partners, and stakeholders. When team members feel valued and respected within their own team, they naturally extend the same courtesy to others outside the organization, forging strong and enduring relationships built on trust and mutual respect.

But perhaps most importantly, encouraging inclusivity within your team has a profound impact on morale and engagement. When individuals feel seen, heard, and valued for who they are, they are more motivated to fully engage with their work and contribute their best efforts. This sense of belonging fosters a deep-seated loyalty to the team and its goals, driving productivity and performance to new heights.

Promoting a culture of inclusivity within your team isn't just the right thing to do—it's a strategic imperative. It unlocks the full potential of every team member, fuels innovation and creativity, and cultivates a sense of belonging that propels the team toward unprecedented success.

Setting Clear Expectations

Importance of Clear Communication

Clear communication serves as the backbone of effective delegation, providing the scaffolding upon which tasks are built and completed. Without clear expectations, team members may find themselves adrift in a sea of uncertainty, unsure of what is required of them and how their contributions fit into the larger picture.

Imagine a scenario where a leader assigns a project without clearly outlining the objectives, timelines, and desired outcomes. Without this crucial information, team members are left to interpret the task on their own, leading to confusion, frustration, and potentially subpar results. Conversely, when expectations are clearly communicated, team members know exactly what is expected of them, enabling them to focus their efforts and deliver on target.

Moreover, clear communication fosters accountability within the team. When expectations are clearly defined, team members understand the parameters of their responsibilities and are more likely to take ownership of their work. This sense of accountability creates a culture of reliability and trust, where team members feel empowered to take initiative and contribute their best efforts.

Furthermore, clear communication helps to mitigate the risk of misunderstandings or errors. By clearly articulating expectations and providing detailed instructions, leaders minimize the potential for misinterpretation and ensure that tasks are completed accurately and efficiently. This not only saves time and resources but also enhances overall productivity and performance within the team.

Clear communication is the linchpin of successful delegation. It provides the clarity and direction necessary for team members to understand their roles and responsibilities, fosters accountability and trust, and minimizes the risk of errors or misunderstandings. By prioritizing clear communication, leaders lay the groundwork for effective delegation and pave the way for success within their teams.

Clarity Varies from Person to Person

Understanding that clarity can vary from person to person is crucial for effective delegation. Each team member has their own preferred style of communication, and what may be clear and concise for one individual could be confusing for another. Leaders must recognize and respect these differences in communication preferences to ensure that instructions are understood and tasks are carried out effectively.

For example, consider a team where some members prefer detailed, step-by-step instructions, while others thrive with more autonomy and flexibility. By acknowledging these differences, leaders can adjust their communication approach to cater to the needs of each team member. This might involve providing more guidance and direction for those who prefer structure while allowing greater freedom and flexibility for those who prefer to work independently.

Moreover, recognizing variability in clarity requires leaders to actively listen and observe how team members respond to instructions. Some team members may readily seek clarification or ask questions when instructions are unclear, while others may hesitate to voice their confusion. Leaders must be attentive to these cues and proactively address any misunderstandings or uncertainties to ensure that all team members are on the same page.

By adapting communication styles to individual preferences, leaders create a more inclusive and collaborative environment within the team. Team members feel valued and respected when their unique communication needs are acknowledged and accommodated, leading to greater engagement and productivity. Additionally, tailoring communication to individual preferences strengthens relationships between leaders and team members, fostering trust and mutual respect.

Tailor Communication and Delegation Styles

Effective delegation hinges not only on clear communication but also on understanding the nuances of individual team members' preferences and communication styles. In essence, what may be crystal clear for one person could be ambiguous for another. Recognizing and adapting to these differences is paramount for successful delegation and team cohesion.

Consider a scenario where a leader assigns a project to two team members, John and Sarah. John thrives on detailed instructions and appreciates regular check-ins to ensure he's on the right track. Sarah, on the other hand, prefers a more hands-off approach, feeling empowered when given the autonomy to tackle tasks in her own way. By tailoring their communication and delegation styles accordingly, the leader can set both John and Sarah up for success while respecting their individual preferences.

Tailoring communication isn't just about customizing instructions— it's about fostering a sense of trust and empowerment within the team. When team members feel understood and respected, they're more likely to be engaged and motivated to excel in their roles. This approach not only enhances productivity but also cultivates a positive work culture where everyone feels valued and supported.

To implement tailored communication effectively, leaders must cultivate strong listening skills and demonstrate empathy toward their team members' needs and preferences. Regular feedback sessions and check-ins provide opportunities to gauge understanding and adjust communication strategies as needed. By fostering open dialogue and transparency, leaders create an environment where team members feel comfortable voicing their concerns and sharing their ideas.

The Importance of Customization

Understand Individual Strengths, Weaknesses, and Areas for Growth

Effective delegation is not just about assigning tasks—it's about knowing your team inside and out. Understanding the strengths, weaknesses, and areas for growth of each team member is paramount for successful delegation. When leaders have a clear understanding of what each team member brings to the table, they can tailor their delegation approach to maximize the potential of the entire team.

First, recognizing individual strengths allows leaders to strategically assign tasks that capitalize on each team member's unique abilities. For example, a team member with strong analytical skills might excel at data-driven tasks, while someone with exceptional creativity could thrive in brainstorming and ideation sessions. By leveraging these strengths, leaders not only ensure that tasks are completed efficiently but also empower team members to work in areas where they shine brightest.

Second, identifying weaknesses provides valuable insights into areas where team members may need additional support or development.

Rather than viewing weaknesses as limitations, leaders can view them as opportunities for growth. For instance, a team member who struggles with public speaking might benefit from opportunities to practice and build confidence in this area. By offering targeted support and resources, leaders can help team members overcome their weaknesses and unlock their full potential.

Furthermore, recognizing areas for growth allows leaders to provide tailored opportunities for development. Whether it's through additional training, mentorship, or stretch assignments, leaders can help team members expand their skill sets and reach new heights in their careers. By investing in their team's professional growth, leaders not only foster a culture of continuous learning but also cultivate a stronger, more resilient team capable of tackling any challenge that comes their way.

Customized Delegation Assignments

Customized delegation assignments are like tailor-made suits—they fit perfectly and make you feel confident and capable. In the realm of delegation, this means assigning tasks that align with each team member's strengths, weaknesses, and growth areas. By customizing delegation assignments, leaders can unlock the full potential of their team members and maximize overall productivity and performance.

When tasks are delegated based on individual strengths, team members are more likely to excel and produce high-quality results. For example, assigning a complex problem-solving task to a team member known for their analytical prowess can lead to innovative solutions and breakthrough insights. Similarly, delegating a creative project to a team member with a flair for design can result in visually stunning and engaging deliverables.

Moreover, customizing delegation assignments provides valuable learning opportunities for team members to develop new skills and expand their capabilities. By delegating tasks that target areas for growth, leaders challenge their team members to step outside their comfort zones and push their boundaries. For instance, assigning a leadership role on a cross-functional project to a team member aspiring to grow into a management position can provide valuable leadership experience and professional development.

Contribution to Overall Team Success

Targeted delegation isn't just about individual achievement—it's about driving collective success. When tasks are delegated strategically based on each team member's strengths and growth areas, the entire team benefits. By maximizing individual potential, leaders create a synergistic team dynamic where each member complements and supports the others.

First, targeted delegation enhances efficiency and effectiveness within the team. When tasks are delegated to those best equipped to handle them, projects move forward smoothly and deadlines are met with ease. This minimizes bottlenecks and delays, allowing the team to operate at peak performance.

Second, targeted delegation fosters collaboration and innovation. When team members are empowered to work in areas where they excel, they bring their unique perspectives and insights to the table. This diversity of thought sparks creativity and drives innovation, leading to better problem-solving and decision-making.

Finally, targeted delegation promotes a culture of trust and accountability within the team. When team members feel that their leader trusts them to handle important tasks, they are more likely to take ownership of their work and deliver results. This sense of trust and accountability strengthens team cohesion and morale, laying the foundation for long-term success.

Conclusion

In this chapter, we've explored the critical aspects of celebrating and leveraging differences within teams. From understanding the importance of recruiting a diverse team to instilling a culture of inclusivity, each element contributes to effective delegation and team success.

Assembling a diverse team isn't just about meeting quotas; it's about harnessing the power of varied backgrounds and perspectives to drive innovation and resilience. By understanding individual strengths, experiences, and perspectives, leaders can tailor their delegation approach to maximize team potential.

Moreover, trust emerges as the foundation of effective delegation. Building trust through understanding and clear communication fosters collaboration and accountability within the team. Recognizing that clarity varies from person to person, leaders must tailor their communication styles to ensure tasks are understood and executed effectively.

Furthermore, customization plays a crucial role in maximizing team potential. By understanding individual strengths, weaknesses, and areas for growth, leaders can assign tasks that challenge and develop team members. Customized delegation assignments contribute to overall team success by empowering each member to excel in their respective roles.

As we conclude this chapter, it's clear that celebrating differences and fostering inclusivity are not just ethical imperatives but strategic advantages. By embracing diversity, building trust, and customizing delegation, leaders create a cohesive and high-performing team poised for success.

Chapter Three

Help Your Employees

In the dynamic world of today's workplaces, there's a vital element often overlooked amid the rush for productivity and efficiency: encouragement. Think of it as the secret sauce that spices up the daily grind, transforming mundane tasks into exciting challenges and fostering a culture where every individual feels valued and empowered.

In this chapter, we delve into the transformative impact of encouragement on individuals and teams, exploring how it ignites motivation, fuels collaboration, and cultivates a thriving work environment. Encouragement isn't just about offering a generic "good job" or a fleeting moment of praise. It's about creating a workplace where every achievement is celebrated, every challenge is met with resilience, and every individual feels inspired to reach their full potential.

Why Encouragement Matters

Impact on Motivation

Encouragement serves as a powerful catalyst for motivation within teams and individuals, driving them toward achieving their goals and exceeding expectations. When individuals receive recognition and praise for their efforts, it validates their hard work and instills a sense of accomplishment. This positive reinforcement not only boosts their confidence but also fuels their desire to continue performing at their best.

Moreover, encouragement acts as a morale booster during challenging times. It serves as a reminder that their contributions are valued and appreciated, even in the face of obstacles. This validation of their efforts motivates individuals to persevere, overcome obstacles, and maintain a positive attitude.

Encouragement also promotes a growth mindset among team members. By acknowledging their progress and efforts, individuals are encouraged to embrace challenges and view failures as opportunities for learning and growth. This mindset shift fosters resilience and perseverance, driving individuals to continually strive for improvement and innovation.

Creating a Positive Work Environment

Encouragement serves as a cornerstone in nurturing a positive work environment characterized by trust, collaboration, and camaraderie. When leaders and peers actively acknowledge and celebrate achievements, it fosters a culture of appreciation and support. Consequently, this cultivates a profound sense of belonging and fulfillment among employees, resulting in heightened levels of job satisfaction and engagement.

A positive work environment fuels creativity and innovation. Encouraging individuals to freely share their ideas and take risks without fear of criticism stimulates out-of-the-box thinking and the proposal of innovative solutions. This culture of openness and encouragement not only amplifies individual creativity but also fosters a collaborative atmosphere where diverse perspectives are embraced and respected.

A positive work environment significantly contributes to employee retention and loyalty. When feeling valued and supported, employees are more inclined to stay committed to their organization, thereby contributing to its long-term success. This reinforcement of bonds between leaders and team members nurtures a deep sense of loyalty and trust, which is crucial for sustained growth and prosperity.

Building Trust and Loyalty

Encouragement serves as a cornerstone in fostering loyalty within organizations, playing a pivotal role in strengthening bonds between leaders and team members. When individuals feel acknowledged and appreciated for their contributions, it cultivates a deep sense of connection and commitment to the organization's mission and values.

First and foremost, encouragement creates a supportive and nurturing environment where employees feel valued and respected. When leaders take the time to recognize and celebrate achievements, it fosters a sense of belonging and loyalty among team members. This validation of their efforts reaffirms their significance within the organization, instilling a strong sense of loyalty and dedication.

Also, encouragement builds trust and rapport between leaders and employees. When individuals receive constructive feedback and praise for their work, it fosters open communication and transparency, laying the foundation for a trusting relationship. This mutual respect and trust are essential for fostering loyalty, as employees feel confident that their contributions are valued and their voices are heard.

Furthermore, encouragement fosters a culture of continuous growth and development. When employees are encouraged to take on new challenges and stretch their capabilities, it creates opportunities for personal and professional growth. This investment in employee development not only enhances job satisfaction but also strengthens loyalty, as employees are more likely to remain committed to an organization that invests in their success.

Strategies for Encouragement

Recognition and Acknowledgment

In the bustling world of business, acknowledgment serves as the fuel that powers the engines of productivity and morale. It's the simple act of recognizing the efforts and contributions of your team members that can turn an ordinary workplace into a thriving hub of motivation and success. Here are some strategies to master the art of recognition:

- **Celebrate Achievements**: Whether it's a small milestone or a major triumph, take the time to celebrate the accomplishments of your team. This could be as simple as a shout-out in a team meeting or a more elaborate recognition ceremony.

- **Personalized Appreciation**: Get to know your team members on a personal level to understand what motivates them. Tailor your acknowledgment to their preferences, whether it's a public commendation or a private word of thanks.

- **Tangible Rewards**: While verbal appreciation goes a long way, tangible rewards can further solidify your recognition efforts. Consider bonuses, extra time off, or even small tokens of appreciation like gift cards or company-branded merchandise.

- **Foster a Culture of Recognition**: Encourage peer-to-peer acknowledgment within your team. When team members acknowledge each other's contributions, it fosters a sense of camaraderie and reinforces the value of teamwork.

- **Timely Recognition**: Don't wait for quarterly reviews or annual appraisals to recognize achievements. Offer immediate feedback and acknowledgment to keep morale high and motivation levels soaring.

Effective Feedback Techniques

Feedback is the lifeblood of growth and improvement within any team. When delivered effectively, feedback has the power to inspire, motivate, and drive positive change. Here are some techniques to master the art of providing constructive feedback:

- **Balance Criticism with Praise**: While it's important to address areas for improvement, don't forget to acknowledge what your team members are doing well. Balancing criticism with praise creates a supportive environment that fosters growth.

- **Encourage Self-Reflection**: Instead of simply telling your team members what they need to improve, encourage them to reflect on their own performance. Ask open-ended questions that prompt self-assessment and problem-solving.

- **Timeliness:** Offer feedback as soon as possible after the event or behavior occurs. This helps ensure that the details are fresh in everyone's minds and allows for timely adjustments if needed.

By mastering these feedback techniques, you can create a culture of continuous improvement where feedback is valued as a catalyst for growth rather than feared as criticism. With effective feedback, you empower your team to learn, adapt, and excel in achieving their goals.

Leading by Example

In the realm of leadership, actions speak louder than words. Leading by example is not just a catchphrase; it's a fundamental principle that sets the tone for the entire organization. Here's why it's crucial and how to embody it effectively:

- **Inspiring Trust and Respect**: When leaders demonstrate the behaviors they expect from their teams, they build trust and respect. Employees are more likely to follow leaders who practice what they preach, fostering a culture of accountability and integrity.

- **Cultivating a Positive Work Environment**: Your behavior sets the standard for acceptable conduct in the workplace. By modeling positivity, professionalism, and resilience, you create an environment where employees feel motivated and empowered to excel.

- **Encouraging Growth and Development**: Leaders who lead by example prioritize continuous improvement and lifelong learning. By demonstrating a commitment to personal and professional growth, they inspire their teams to do the same, fostering a culture of innovation and adaptability.

- **Strengthening Team Cohesion**: Actions speak volumes about a leader's values and priorities. When leaders consistently demonstrate empathy, collaboration, and inclusivity, they foster a sense of belonging and unity within the team, driving collective success.

- **Resolving Conflict Effectively**: During times of conflict or adversity, leaders who lead by example can defuse tensions and promote constructive dialogue. By modeling effective communication, empathy, and conflict-resolution skills, they guide their teams toward resolution and reconciliation.

The Psychological Benefits and Productivity Boost

Understanding the Psychological Impact

Encouragement isn't just a feel-good gesture; it's a powerful tool that taps into the core of human psychology, driving motivation and productivity. At its essence, encouragement validates an individual's efforts, fostering a sense of value and belonging in the workplace.

One psychological theory that elucidates the impact of encouragement is self-determination theory (SDT). According to SDT, humans have three basic psychological needs: autonomy, competence, and relatedness. Encouragement addresses these needs by empowering employees to make decisions (autonomy), recognizing their skills and efforts (competence), and fostering positive connections within the team (relatedness). When these needs are met, individuals are more intrinsically motivated to perform at their best.

Moreover, encouragement triggers the release of neurotransmitters such as dopamine and serotonin in the brain, leading to feelings of happiness and fulfillment. This neurochemical response reinforces positive behaviors, creating a cycle of increased productivity and well-being.

Furthermore, social cognitive theory posits that individuals learn and model behaviors through observation and reinforcement. When leaders provide consistent encouragement, they serve as role models, influencing employees to emulate proactive and engaged behaviors.

Understanding these psychological underpinnings highlights the profound impact of encouragement on employee morale and productivity.

By cultivating a culture of support and recognition, organizations can harness the full potential of their workforce to achieve remarkable results.

Quantifying the Productivity Boost

The correlation between employee happiness, encouragement, and productivity is not merely anecdotal; it is supported by a wealth of empirical evidence. Numerous studies have delved into the intricate relationship between workplace encouragement and its tangible effects on organizational performance.

For instance, research conducted by Gallup, a global analytics and advisory firm and a creator of a workplace performance platform, consistently demonstrates a strong link between employee engagement and productivity. In one study, highly engaged teams showed a 21 percent increase in profitability compared to their less engaged counterparts. Moreover, organizations with engaged employees experience lower turnover rates and higher customer satisfaction, translating into substantial financial gains.

A meta-analysis published by Timothy A. Judge and Gerald R. Ferris in the *Journal of Applied* Psychology in 1993, found that positive reinforcement strategies, such as praise and recognition, have a significant impact on employee performance and motivation. Employees who receive regular encouragement are more likely to exhibit higher levels of job satisfaction, commitment, and discretionary effort.

Studies examining the role of neurotransmitters in motivation and productivity reveal that positive feedback triggers the release of dopamine, enhancing cognitive function and problem-solving abilities. This neurological response not only boosts individual performance but also fosters a collaborative and innovative work environment.

The empirical data unequivocally supports the notion that encouragement is a catalyst for enhanced productivity and organizational success. By quantifying the productivity boost associated with encouragement, organizations can make informed decisions to prioritize employee well-being and cultivate a culture of positivity and achievement.

Case Studies and Success Stories

Real-life examples of organizations that have implemented encouragement strategies and witnessed tangible productivity gains serve as compelling evidence of the effectiveness of such approaches.

One notable case is that of Zappos, the online shoe and clothing retailer renowned for its exceptional customer service culture. Zappos places a strong emphasis on employee happiness and empowerment, offering extensive training and development programs alongside a supportive work environment. Through initiatives like "Zapponian of the Month" awards and peer recognition programs, Zappos fosters a culture of encouragement and appreciation. As a result, the company consistently ranks among the top performers in customer satisfaction metrics, demonstrating the direct correlation between employee morale and customer experience.

Another example comes from Google, a global technology giant known for its innovative and dynamic workplace culture. Google encourages a culture of psychological safety, where employees feel empowered to take risks and share ideas without fear of criticism. Through initiatives like "20 percent time," where employees are encouraged to dedicate a portion of their work hours to personal projects, Google has fostered a culture of creativity and innovation. This encouragement of autonomy and experimentation has led to the development of groundbreaking products such as Gmail and Google Maps, highlighting the transformative power of encouragement on organizational innovation and productivity.

These case studies underscore the tangible benefits of implementing encouragement strategies in the workplace. By prioritizing employee well-being and fostering a culture of support and recognition, organizations can unlock the full potential of their workforce, driving productivity, innovation, and, ultimately, success.

Implementing Positive Changes for Future Generations

Offering Flexible Work Arrangements

Embracing flexibility in the workplace is no longer just a trend—it's a necessity. Recognizing the diverse lifestyles and commitments of your employees, offering flexible work arrangements can be a game-changer in fostering a thriving and inclusive work culture. Let's delve into some key facets of flexible work arrangements:

- **Remote Work Options**: The advent of technology has revolutionized the way we work, making remote work more feasible and advantageous than ever before. By allowing employees to work from the comfort of their homes or any location of their choice, businesses can unlock a myriad of benefits. From heightened productivity to increased job satisfaction and reduced overhead costs, the advantages of remote work are undeniable. Moreover, offering remote work options demonstrates trust in your employees' ability to deliver results autonomously, fostering a sense of empowerment and accountability.

- **Flexible Schedules**: Traditional 9-to-5 schedules may not align with the diverse needs and responsibilities of your workforce. Enter flexible scheduling—a paradigm that empowers employees to customize their work hours based on individual preferences and obligations. Whether it's accommodating childcare responsibilities, pursuing further education, or simply optimizing productivity during peak hours, flexible schedules afford employees the autonomy to strike a harmonious balance between work and personal life. By prioritizing employee well-being and work-life balance, businesses can cultivate a more engaged and loyal workforce.

- **Compressed Workweeks**: Imagine condensing a standard five-day workweek into fewer days without compromising productivity or quality of work. Enter compressed workweeks—an innovative approach to scheduling that offers employees the opportunity to work longer hours over fewer days. By compressing their work schedule, employees can enjoy extended weekends and more uninterrupted time for personal pursuits. This not only enhances work-life balance but also contributes to reduced stress levels and heightened job satisfaction. Embracing compressed workweeks exemplifies a commitment to employee-centric policies that prioritize holistic well-being and foster a culture of trust and flexibility.

Implementing Incentive Programs

Motivation is the fuel that drives exceptional performance and fosters a culture of excellence within your organization. Incentive programs serve as powerful tools for recognizing and rewarding the hard work and dedication of your employees. Let's explore the key components of implementing effective incentive programs:

- **Recognition Programs**: Acknowledgment is a fundamental human need, and recognition programs play a pivotal role in fulfilling this need within the workplace. By publicly celebrating achievements, milestones, and contributions, recognition programs not only boost morale but also reinforce positive behaviors and values. Whether it's a simple shout-out in a team meeting or a prestigious award ceremony, recognizing employees for their efforts cultivates a culture of appreciation and motivates individuals to strive for excellence.

- **Bonus Structures**: Incentivizing high performance through bonus structures is a tried-and-true method for driving productivity and results. From performance-based bonuses to profit-sharing schemes, there are various approaches to designing bonus structures that align with your organizational goals and values. By tying financial rewards to individual or team achievements, bonus structures incentivize employees to go above and beyond their duties, driving innovation and fostering a culture of continuous improvement.

- **Perks and Benefits**: Beyond monetary rewards, perks and benefits serve as valuable incentives for attracting and retaining top talent while nurturing employee loyalty. From flexible work arrangements and wellness programs to professional development opportunities and company retreats, the options for perks and benefits are endless. By offering tailored perks that cater to the diverse needs and preferences of your workforce, you demonstrate a commitment to employee well-being and satisfaction, ultimately fostering a more engaged and loyal team.

Fostering Collaboration and Teamwork

In today's interconnected and fast-paced work environment, collaboration and teamwork are not just buzzwords—they are essential ingredients for driving innovation, solving complex problems, and achieving collective success. Let's explore how you can cultivate a culture of collaboration and teamwork within your organization:

- **Encouraging Open Communication**: Effective communication lies at the heart of collaboration and teamwork. By fostering open communication channels, you create an environment where ideas can flow freely, feedback is valued, and misunderstandings are minimized. Encourage transparency, active listening, and constructive dialogue among team members to foster trust and build strong relationships. Whether it's through regular team meetings, town halls, or digital platforms, prioritize open communication as a cornerstone of your organizational culture.

- **Facilitating Cross-Functional Projects**: Silos inhibit collaboration and innovation within organizations. Break down these barriers by facilitating cross-functional projects that bring together individuals from different departments or disciplines. Cross-functional collaboration not only promotes diverse perspectives and creative problem-solving but also fosters a culture of mutual respect and appreciation for varied skill sets. Encourage teams to collaborate across boundaries to tackle challenges, drive change, and deliver impactful results that transcend traditional departmental boundaries.

- **Organizing Team-Building Activities**: Strong teams are built on trust, camaraderie, and a shared sense of purpose. Organizing team-building activities provides opportunities for team members to connect on a personal level, strengthen bonds, and foster a sense of belonging. From outdoor retreats and volunteer initiatives to team lunches and virtual social events, there are countless ways to cultivate a positive team dynamic and nurture a supportive work culture. By investing in team-building activities, you not only boost morale and motivation but also lay the foundation for long-term collaboration and success.

Conclusion

In the realm of modern workplaces, the significance of encouragement cannot be overstated. Throughout Chapter 3, "Help Your Employees," we've embarked on a journey to explore the multifaceted impact of encouragement on individuals, teams, and organizations. From igniting motivation to fostering collaboration and nurturing loyalty, encouragement serves as the cornerstone of a thriving work culture where every individual feels valued and empowered.

By recognizing the importance of encouragement, we've uncovered its transformative power in creating a positive work environment where trust, respect, and camaraderie flourish. Through strategies such as recognition and acknowledgment, effective feedback techniques, and leading by example, leaders can cultivate a culture of encouragement that inspires greatness and drives success.

Furthermore, our exploration into the psychological benefits of encouragement has shed light on its profound impact on employee morale and productivity. By understanding the underlying mechanisms that drive motivation and well-being, organizations can harness the full potential of their workforce to achieve remarkable results.

As we look to the future, implementing positive changes such as offering flexible work arrangements, implementing incentive programs, and fostering collaboration and teamwork will be instrumental in creating workplaces where individuals thrive and organizations prosper. By prioritizing encouragement as a guiding principle, we pave the way for a brighter, more inclusive, and more fulfilling work environment for future generations.

In closing, let us remember that encouragement isn't just a fleeting gesture; it's a catalyst for growth, innovation, and success. By championing encouragement in our workplaces, we unlock the potential of every individual to make meaningful contributions and create a better tomorrow for all.

Furthermore, purposeful delegation involves a thoughtful consideration of individual strengths, skills, and developmental needs. Leaders must recognize that each member of their team brings unique talents and expertise to the table. By assigning tasks that capitalize on these strengths, leaders not only maximize efficiency and productivity but also empower team members to excel in their roles. Moreover, purposeful delegation presents an opportunity for professional growth and development. By delegating tasks that challenge and stretch team members, leaders foster a culture of continuous learning and improvement, ensuring that their team remains agile and adaptable in the face of change.

Crucially, purposeful delegation is grounded in trust and empowerment. Leaders must trust their team members to execute tasks effectively and make decisions autonomously. This trust forms the foundation of a strong and resilient team, where individuals feel valued, respected, and motivated to contribute their best work. Empowerment goes hand in hand with trust, as leaders provide their team members with the resources, support, and autonomy needed to succeed. By empowering team members to take ownership of their work, leaders foster a sense of accountability and ownership, driving motivation and engagement.

Purposeful delegation also involves ongoing communication and feedback. Leaders must ensure that expectations are clear, goals are understood, and progress is monitored effectively. Regular check-ins provide an opportunity for leaders to offer support and guidance, address any challenges or concerns, and celebrate achievements along the way. Moreover, open communication fosters a culture of transparency and collaboration, where ideas are shared, feedback is welcomed, and solutions are co-created.

Use the Eisenhower Matrix

Introduction to the Eisenhower Matrix

Developed by President Dwight D. Eisenhower, this decision-making tool provides a structured approach to prioritizing tasks based on their urgency and importance. In today's fast-paced world, where leaders are inundated with competing demands, mastering the art of delegation is essential for maintaining productivity and achieving strategic objectives. By understanding and leveraging the Eisenhower Matrix, leaders can streamline their delegation process and focus their efforts on tasks that yield the greatest impact. Throughout this chapter, we'll explore how the Eisenhower Matrix can serve as a valuable resource for leaders seeking to optimize their delegation practices and achieve greater effectiveness.

Understand Urgency and Importance

Before we explore the intricacies of the Eisenhower Matrix, let's clarify the fundamental concepts of urgency and importance. Urgent tasks demand immediate attention, often driven by external pressures or deadlines. These tasks require swift action to prevent negative consequences or capitalize on time-sensitive opportunities. Importance, on the other hand, refers to the significance of a task in contributing to long-term goals or objectives. Important tasks may not be time-sensitive, but neglecting them can have far-reaching implications for organizational success. By discerning between urgency and importance, leaders can make informed decisions about task prioritization and delegation, ensuring that critical objectives are not overshadowed by immediate demands.

Application of the Eisenhower Matrix for Delegation

Now that we've established a foundation, let's discuss how leaders can leverage the Eisenhower Matrix to enhance their delegation practices. The colleagues for awards or shout-outs based on specific criteria, such as demonstrating company values or going above and beyond in their roles.

- **Appreciation Days or Weeks**: Designate specific days or weeks throughout the year to celebrate appreciation and recognition within the organization. This could involve organizing special events, activities, or team-building exercises centered around gratitude and appreciation, fostering a positive and supportive work environment.

Cultivating Traditions

Cultivating traditions around appreciation provides meaningful opportunities for team members to come together and celebrate shared values, achievements, and milestones. These traditions create a sense of continuity and belonging within the organization, fostering a strong sense of community and camaraderie among team members. Examples of appreciation traditions include:

- **Annual Awards Ceremonies**: Host an annual awards ceremony to recognize and celebrate outstanding performers, top achievers, and individuals who exemplify the organization's values and mission. This could involve presenting awards or trophies, sharing success stories, and expressing gratitude for the contributions of award recipients.

- **Team-Building Events**: Organize regular team-building events or activities that incorporate elements of appreciation and recognition. This could include team outings, volunteer opportunities, or group exercises aimed at fostering teamwork, collaboration, and mutual support.

- **Special Celebrations**: Mark significant milestones, such as the company's anniversary, project milestones, or employee birthdays, with special celebrations and events. This could involve organizing parties, luncheons, or other social gatherings where team members can come together to celebrate achievements and express appreciation for one another.

Overcoming Challenges in Expressing Appreciation

Addressing Cultural Differences

- **Cultural Awareness Training**: Organizing cultural awareness training sessions can help team members understand and appreciate the diverse cultural backgrounds present within the organization. These sessions can cover topics such as communication styles, attitudes toward hierarchy, and expressions of appreciation common in different cultures. By increasing cultural competency among team members, misunderstandings and misinterpretations related to appreciation can be minimized.

- **Tailored Approaches**: Recognizing that one size does not fit all when it comes to appreciation, leaders should adapt their approaches based on the preferences and norms of different cultural groups within the team. This may involve conducting surveys or focus groups to gather insights on how team members from different cultural backgrounds prefer to give and receive recognition. Tailoring appreciation practices to align with cultural norms allows leaders to ensure that their gestures of appreciation are well-received and meaningful to all team members.

- **Open Communication**: Creating an environment of open communication where team members feel comfortable discussing cultural differences is crucial. Leaders should encourage dialogue and provide opportunities for team members to share their perspectives and experiences related to appreciation. This can help build understanding and empathy among team members and foster a culture of inclusivity and respect.

Overcoming Barriers

- **Leadership Support**: Leadership buy-in is essential for the success of any appreciation initiative. Leaders at all levels of the organization should actively support and participate in appreciation initiatives, leading by example. When leaders demonstrate a genuine commitment to appreciation, it sends a powerful message to the rest of the team and helps overcome resistance to change.

- **Clear Communication**: Effective communication is key to overcoming barriers related to appreciation. Leaders should clearly communicate the importance of appreciation and recognition to all team members, emphasizing how it contributes to employee morale, engagement, and organizational success. Addressing any misconceptions or concerns that may arise and providing regular updates on appreciation initiatives can help build trust and buy-in among team members.

- **Flexibility**: Flexibility is crucial when it comes to implementing appreciation initiatives. Leaders should be willing to adapt their approaches based on feedback and evolving organizational needs. This may involve experimenting with different appreciation practices, soliciting input from team members, and making adjustments as needed. By remaining flexible and responsive to the changing needs of the organization, leaders can overcome barriers and ensure the success of appreciation initiatives.

Sustaining Momentum

- **Regular Feedback**: Soliciting feedback from team members is essential for sustaining momentum in appreciation initiatives. Leaders should regularly seek input from team members to assess the effectiveness of appreciation practices and identify areas for improvement. This can involve conducting surveys, holding focus groups, or implementing suggestion boxes to gather feedback on what is working well and where there is room for enhancement.

- **Integration into Organizational Culture**: Embedding appreciation into the organizational culture is critical for sustaining momentum over time. Leaders should ensure that appreciation becomes a natural part of everyday interactions and is reflected in the organization's values and norms. This may involve incorporating appreciation into performance management processes, recognition programs, and leadership development initiatives. Integrating appreciation into the organizational culture helps leaders create a workplace where team members feel valued, motivated, and engaged.

Identifying Key Metrics

Determining relevant metrics to evaluate the effectiveness of appreciation efforts is crucial for assessing their impact on employee morale, engagement, and organizational performance. Some key metrics for evaluating appreciation efforts may include:

- **Employee Satisfaction**: Measure employee satisfaction levels through surveys or feedback mechanisms to assess how appreciated employees feel within the organization. Look for trends in satisfaction scores related to recognition and appreciation practices to identify areas for improvement.

- **Employee Engagement**: Track employee engagement levels, such as participation in company events, willingness to go above and beyond in their roles, and overall commitment to the organization. Higher levels of engagement are often associated with effective appreciation efforts.

- **Employee Retention**: Monitor employee turnover rates and retention rates to gauge the impact of appreciation initiatives on employee retention. A positive correlation between appreciation and employee retention suggests that employees feel valued and are more likely to stay with the organization.

- **Productivity and Performance**: Assess changes in productivity and performance metrics, such as individual and team performance ratings, project completion rates, and key performance indicators. Improved performance outcomes may indicate that appreciation initiatives are motivating employees to perform at their best.

By identifying and tracking these key metrics, leaders can gain insights into the effectiveness of appreciation efforts and make informed decisions to optimize their impact. Regularly reviewing and analyzing these metrics allows leaders to identify areas for improvement and adjust appreciation strategies accordingly, ensuring that employees feel valued, motivated, and engaged within the organization.

Conclusion

Throughout this chapter, we've seen that "The Art of Appreciation" is not just about acknowledging contributions; it's about cultivating an environment where gratitude thrives, motivation soars, and individuals flourish. In this chapter, we've explored the transformative power of appreciation and its multifaceted impact on employee morale, motivation, and performance.

From the seemingly small acts of saying "thank you" to the systematic implementation of recognition programs, each gesture of appreciation serves to validate the efforts of individuals within the organization. We've seen how recognition not only boosts morale but also cultivates a sense of belonging and commitment among employees. Moreover, we've examined how expressing gratitude acts as a catalyst for motivation, inspiring individuals to go above and beyond in their roles and contributing to the overall success of the organization.

But appreciation isn't just about praise and recognition; it also involves providing constructive criticism aimed at fostering growth and development. We've delved into the significance of constructive criticism and offered strategies for delivering feedback effectively, ensuring that individuals receive actionable insights that facilitate their personal and professional advancement.

Furthermore, we've explored the diverse forms of rewards and recognition, from tangible incentives to nonmonetary gestures, and examined their role in reinforcing desired behaviors and values within the organization. By celebrating milestones and establishing rituals and traditions centered around appreciation, leaders can create a workplace culture where individuals feel valued, supported, and motivated to excel.

However, expressing appreciation is not without its challenges. We've addressed how leaders can navigate cultural differences and overcome barriers to ensure that appreciation efforts are inclusive and effective. Finally, we've discussed the importance of identifying key metrics to evaluate the impact of appreciation initiatives, enabling leaders to make data-driven decisions to optimize their effectiveness over time.

In conclusion, as leaders embrace the art of appreciation, they not only cultivate a positive work culture but also lay the foundation for long-term success and sustainability in their organizations.

Conclusion

As we reach the conclusion of our journey through *Delegate like a Boss*, it's a moment to pause and reflect on the transformation you've undergone as a leader. Throughout these chapters, you've learned so much about effective delegation, which will help you to improve your skills and empower your team to achieve greatness.

We bid farewell to these pages, but remember that it's not just an ending— it's a new beginning. Armed with the knowledge and insights gleaned from this journey, you're equipped to step boldly into the future of leadership. It's time to embrace your role as a visionary, a mentor, and a catalyst for change.

As you venture forth, remember that delegation isn't just a tool in your leadership arsenal—it's a mindset, a philosophy, and a guiding principle. It's about trusting in your team, empowering them to take ownership, and instituting a culture of collaboration and innovation.

So, when navigating the complexities of leadership, keep these principles close to your heart. Lead with empathy, courage, and integrity. Celebrate the diversity of thought and talent within your team, and never underestimate the power of collective effort.

As you bid adieu to these pages, carry with you the lessons learned and the wisdom gained. Reflect on the journey you've traveled and the milestones you've achieved. But more importantly, look ahead to the future with optimism and determination.

For the journey of leadership is a never-ending one, filled with twists and turns, challenges and triumphs. But through it all, remember that you are not alone. You have a team—a family—standing beside you, ready to support you, challenge you, and celebrate with you every step of the way.

Most importantly, you have to always remember: the greatest leaders aren't just remembered for what they achieve themselves—they're remembered for the lives they touch, the teams they build, and the legacy they leave behind.